Acting Edition

Paris

by Clara Mamet

‖SAMUEL FRENCH‖

Copyright © 2012 by Clara Mamet
All Rights Reserved

PARIS is fully protected under the copyright laws of the United States of America, the British Commonwealth, including Canada, and all member countries of the Berne Convention for the Protection of Literary and Artistic Works, the Universal Copyright Convention, and/or the World Trade Organization conforming to the Agreement on Trade Related Aspects of Intellectual Property Rights. All rights, including professional and amateur stage productions, recitation, lecturing, public reading, motion picture, radio broadcasting, television, online/digital production, and the rights of translation into foreign languages are strictly reserved.

ISBN 978-0-573-70068-2

www.concordtheatricals.com
www.concordtheatricals.co.uk

FOR PRODUCTION INQUIRIES

UNITED STATES AND CANADA
info@concordtheatricals.com
1-866-979-0447

UNITED KINGDOM AND EUROPE
licensing@concordtheatricals.co.uk
020-7054-7298

Each title is subject to availability from Concord Theatricals Corp., depending upon country of performance. Please be aware that *PARIS* may not be licensed by Concord Theatricals Corp. in your territory. Professional and amateur producers should contact the nearest Concord Theatricals Corp. office or licensing partner to verify availability.

CAUTION: Professional and amateur producers are hereby warned that *PARIS* is subject to a licensing fee. The purchase, renting, lending or use of this book does not constitute a license to perform this title(s), which license must be obtained from Concord Theatricals Corp. prior to any performance. Performance of this title(s) without a license is a violation of federal law and may subject the producer and/or presenter of such performances to civil penalties. Both amateurs and professionals considering a production are strongly advised to apply to the appropriate agent before starting rehearsals, advertising, or booking a theatre. A licensing fee must be paid whether the title(s) is presented for charity or gain and whether or not admission is charged. Professional/Stock licensing fees are quoted upon application to Concord Theatricals Corp.

This work is published by Samuel French, an imprint of Concord Theatricals Corp.

No one shall make any changes in this title(s) for the purpose of production. No part of this book may be reproduced, stored in a retrieval system, scanned, uploaded, or transmitted in any form, by any means, now known or yet to be invented, including mechanical, electronic, digital, photocopying, recording, videotaping, or otherwise, without the prior written permission of the publisher. No one shall share this title(s), or any part of this title(s), through any social media or file hosting websites.

For all inquiries regarding motion picture, television, online/digital and other media rights, please contact Concord Theatricals Corp.

MUSIC AND THIRD-PARTY MATERIALS USE NOTE

Licensees are solely responsible for obtaining formal written permission from copyright owners to use copyrighted music and/or other copyrighted third-party materials (e.g. artworks, logos) in the performance of this play and are strongly cautioned to do so. If no such permission is obtained by the licensee, then the licensee must use only original music and materials that the licensee owns and controls. Licensees are solely responsible and liable for clearances of all third-party copyrighted materials, including without limitation music, and shall indemnify the copyright owners of the play(s) and their licensing agent, Concord Theatricals Corp., against any costs, expenses, losses and liabilities arising from the use of such copyrighted third-party materials by licensees. For music, please contact the appropriate music licensing authority in your territory for the rights to any incidental music.

IMPORTANT BILLING AND CREDIT REQUIREMENTS

If you have obtained performance rights to this title, please refer to your licensing agreement for important billing and credit requirements.

PARIS opened in a world premiere production on April 13, 2012 at the Ruskin Group Theatre Company in Santa Monica, California. The evening of the two one acts was produced by John Ruskin, Artistic Director; Michael Meyers, Managing Director; and Mike Reilly, Production Manager. The production was directed by Paul Sand. The cast was as follows:

DAUGHTER . . . . Clara Mamet
FATHER . . . . John Pirruccello

CHARACTERS

FATHER - A man, late forties-late fifties.
DAUGHTER - A girl, mid teens-mid twenties.

SET

A table and two chairs. There is a coffee pot on top of the table.

FATHER. I woke up this morning, looked out my window and–

DAUGHTER. Would you like some coffee?

FATHER. What? No. I woke up this morning–

DAUGHTER. I just made it.

FATHER. Can you think of anything more monotonous?

DAUGHTER. Coffee?

FATHER. No, no, not the coffee, I'm telling you I woke up this morning, looked out my window, and–

DAUGHTER. It's good coffee – what?

FATHER. What?

DAUGHTER. You woke up this morning, looked out your window and what?

FATHER. That's all, that's what I'm trying to tell you. Monotony, monotony, monotony, it gets so vastly monotonous.

DAUGHTER. Well, what happened then?

FATHER. What happened then, what?

DAUGHTER. What happened when you looked out your window?

FATHER. Nothing, that's just what I mean.

DAUGHTER. Ah, I see.

FATHER. Since when have you made coffee?

DAUGHTER. I don't know, I couldn't sleep.

FATHER. Well, why not?

DAUGHTER. So many reasons.

FATHER. Really?

DAUGHTER. No. A boy.

FATHER. Ah.

DAUGHTER. An idiot boy doesn't like me.

FATHER. Well, that's alright, I'm sure there are many fine people who don't like you.

DAUGHTER. I mean he doesn't love me.

FATHER. Ah. Well then he's an idiot, as you say.

DAUGHTER. Yes, but you see that's not the point.

FATHER. Well, how do you know he doesn't love you?

DAUGHTER. I asked him, he said no.

FATHER. Well again, as you have rightly pointed out, an idiot.

DAUGHTER. Yes, but oddly that doesn't seem to help.

FATHER. Ah.

DAUGHTER. So I made a pot of coffee.

FATHER. Did that help?

DAUGHTER. Not particularly.

FATHER. You know my dear, whenever I stumble upon a fork in the road I always find it helpful to ask myself, "What would *I* do?"

DAUGHTER. And what do you tell yourself?

FATHER. It depends on the situation.

DAUGHTER. So what would you tell yourself in this situation?

FATHER. I wouldn't know all the boys I know are madly in love with me.

DAUGHTER. I suppose it's to be expected.

FATHER. Mm.

DAUGHTER. A pretty young thing like you?

FATHER. Yes. You say he doesn't love you?

DAUGHTER. That's right.

FATHER. Well, why the hell not?

DAUGHTER. He says he doesn't want a relationship.

FATHER. Oh. Well then he's a bigger fool than I thought.

DAUGHTER. What does that mean, "I don't want a relationship?"

FATHER. It means, "I'm a fool and I don't like being nice to women."

DAUGHTER. But he's nice enough.

FATHER. Well, apparently not. What flavor coffee?

DAUGHTER. Coffee should never have a flavor.

FATHER. Quite right.

DAUGHTER. Coffee is coffee flavored, anything else is just a hot slushee.

FATHER. You're a very wise young woman.

DAUGHTER. I know.

FATHER. You're a very wise young woman so why are you hanging around with a fool?

DAUGHTER. Well, perhaps I like being unhappy.

FATHER. No, no, that's too easy.

DAUGHTER. Well perhaps I've nothing else to do.

FATHER. No, that isn't it.

DAUGHTER. Isn't it?

FATHER. No, you're too smart for that.

DAUGHTER. Well, what then?

FATHER. He hurt your pride.

DAUGHTER. Yes, he hurt my pride.

FATHER. I see. So you don't really love him you just want him to love you?

DAUGHTER. Why shouldn't I want him to love me? Why shouldn't he love me?

FATHER. He should, but you see you don't love him.

DAUGHTER. No.

FATHER. So it makes it easier to forget him.

DAUGHTER. I suppose.

FATHER. Your pride's just hurt.

DAUGHTER. Yes.

FATHER. It shouldn't be.

DAUGHTER. Whys that?

FATHER. You're too smart to hang around with guys that are stupid enough not to love you.

DAUGHTER. Hmmm…

FATHER. But you'd like to be in love.

DAUGHTER. Yes, I'd like to be in love.

FATHER. You're upset because you're not in love.

DAUGHTER. Yes.

FATHER. I bet if that idiot boy would stop being an idiot he would love you.

DAUGHTER. Maybe.

FATHER. But then he wouldn't "be himself," which seems so important to the youth these days.

DAUGHTER. Yes.

FATHER. You wouldn't love him even if he stopped being an idiot.

DAUGHTER. Yes, yes, I suppose you're right.

FATHER. I was one of those once.

DAUGHTER. An idiot?

FATHER. Mm.

DAUGHTER. Then what happened?

FATHER. I got older. Fell in love.

DAUGHTER. And how was that?

FATHER. Better than being an idiot.

DAUGHTER. It seems like it would be.

FATHER. Yes.

DAUGHTER. It seems nice.

FATHER. Yes.

DAUGHTER. Sometimes I imagine that my one true love pledges his life to me and he dies in a tragic accident and I'm left a ruined woman for the end of my days.

FATHER. Hm…

DAUGHTER. And that's what I'd like to be.

FATHER. A ruined woman for the end of your days?

DAUGHTER. Yes. Crying and staring out windows all the time. And people would say, "Look at that terribly sad, terribly beautiful woman, she suffered a great loss in her youth." And then they'd keep walking. That's what I'd like to be.

FATHER. In theory, not in practice.

DAUGHTER. No I really would. I would like to shut myself up in my room and sleep all day long, forever a wounded heart.

FATHER. That's not a wounded heart, that's a teenager.

DAUGHTER. Maybe.

FATHER. Why a wounded heart?

DAUGHTER. Because it's better to have loved and lost than–

FATHER. Yes, but why would you want him to die in the first place?

DAUGHTER. For the attention.

FATHER. *(laughs)* I see. You're very funny.

DAUGHTER. I'm glad you think so.

FATHER. I do.

DAUGHTER. High praise indeed.

FATHER. Chin-up.

DAUGHTER. You think so?

FATHER. I do.

(beat)

DAUGHTER. Why is nothing outside your window monotonous?

FATHER. Because there's always nothing there, which is the definition of monotony.

DAUGHTER. I see.

FATHER. It is unchanging.

DAUGHTER. I understand.

FATHER. It's not just the window.

DAUGHTER. Ah.

FATHER. I'm lonely, you see.

DAUGHTER. Me too.

FATHER. You're not lonely.

DAUGHTER. Why not?

FATHER. Young people are never lonely.

DAUGHTER. Why's that?

FATHER. You have the youth to keep you company.

DAUGHTER. Don't you have the old?

FATHER. They're dead.

DAUGHTER. Oh.

FATHER. I miss your mother, you see.

DAUGHTER. I know you do.

FATHER. Because I loved her.

DAUGHTER. And is it better to have loved and lost than never to have loved at all?

FATHER. Well I would have preferred it if she hadn't died.

DAUGHTER. She didn't die.

FATHER. It feels the same. The flaw in your fantasy you see, is that when you love someone you tend to want them to stay alive.

DAUGHTER. I understand, I'm sorry that you miss her.

FATHER. Thank you.

DAUGHTER. I'm sorry that she left.

FATHER. I know you are.

(beat)

DAUGHTER. I'm tired.

FATHER. It's understandable.

DAUGHTER. I didn't get much sleep.

FATHER. Precisely.

DAUGHTER. Sometimes, I get too bored to sleep.

FATHER. I know what you mean. They're similar aren't they?

DAUGHTER. What?

FATHER. Boredom and loneliness.

DAUGHTER. Are they?

FATHER. They are the same in that one can create the other and vice versa.

DAUGHTER. That's true.

FATHER. And with both you are doing virtually the same thing. The distinction with loneliness is that you're sad, whereas with boredom you're just bored.

DAUGHTER. That's very apt.
FATHER. I've thought a lot about it.
DAUGHTER. Are you unhappy?
FATHER. Being unhappy is a goddamn shame.
DAUGHTER. I think that's why they call it "being unhappy."
FATHER. I like you very much.
DAUGHTER. Thank you.
FATHER. I'm proud of the way you've grown up.
DAUGHTER. I appreciate that.
FATHER. Mostly because you remind me of myself.
DAUGHTER. I know.
FATHER. And in that, we are alike.

   (beat)

DAUGHTER. Why don't you switch rooms?
FATHER. What?
DAUGHTER. The view in your room, you say it's monotonous, why don't you switch?
FATHER. Thank you, I will.
DAUGHTER. What?
FATHER. Switch rooms, you're absolutely right.
DAUGHTER. Why didn't you before?
FATHER. What?
DAUGHTER. You're smart, why didn't you switch rooms before?
FATHER. Because I'm a grumpy old curmudgeon and I like complaining.
DAUGHTER. Well that makes sense.
FATHER. But you're absolutely right.
DAUGHTER. Well, I just thought–
FATHER. It's quite valid.
DAUGHTER. Since, as you very correctly say, "Being unhappy *is* a goddamn shame."
FATHER. Yes my dear, you're quite right.
DAUGHTER. Well–

FATHER. No, no. I have once again been outsmarted by a woman. I know better than to not take your advice.

DAUGHTER. Thank you.

FATHER. You're welcome.

(beat)

DAUGHTER. Do you suppose it's a full moon?

FATHER. Well, that's a good question.

DAUGHTER. Hmm…

FATHER. It could very well be.

DAUGHTER. Yeah.

FATHER. I wouldn't know, I don't read lunar reports.

DAUGHTER. Nor do I.

FATHER. Ah.

DAUGHTER. Would you like to know why?

FATHER. Why's that?

DAUGHTER. Because I'm not a douchebag.

FATHER. Very good.

DAUGHTER. Well–

FATHER. Still…

DAUGHTER. Yes?

FATHER. I knew a man once, said the only time he ever knew anything was when he was looking at a full moon.

DAUGHTER. And?

FATHER. He was blind, and he was an idiot.

DAUGHTER. But still.

FATHER. Yes?

DAUGHTER. He was right about the one thing he knew.

FATHER. Yes.

DAUGHTER. And in that, one hundred percent of his theories were correct.

FATHER. Very true.

DAUGHTER. I suppose that's the beauty of sight, isn't it?

FATHER. What?

DAUGHTER. You can see things.
FATHER. Oh very good, very good.

(beat)

FATHER. Are *you* unhappy?
DAUGHTER. Not particularly.
FATHER. But shouldn't you be off with your friends?
DAUGHTER. I don't have any friends.
FATHER. Ah, well done.
DAUGHTER. I'm the greatest company I'll ever find. Do you?
FATHER. Do I, what?
DAUGHTER. Have friends?
FATHER. No.
DAUGHTER. Why not?
FATHER. Similar reasons. Also one can rarely get in fights with oneself.
DAUGHTER. No. One does, though.
FATHER. One does what?
DAUGHTER. Get in fights with oneself.
FATHER. Certainly, it's called indigestion.
DAUGHTER. Yes, but you know what I mean. One does…
FATHER. One does what?
DAUGHTER. Get in fights with oneself.
FATHER. Does one?
DAUGHTER. I think so.
FATHER. In what sense?
DAUGHTER. Mind versus spirit.
FATHER. Yes, but can you give it a name? What would you say it's equal to?
DAUGHTER. The ability to make a decision.
FATHER. Ah.
DAUGHTER. The ability to make a decision is a fight with oneself.

FATHER. Yes, I see.

DAUGHTER. The ability to–

FATHER. To decide to be happy again, I understand.

DAUGHTER. Yes.

FATHER. The ability to force yourself to have fun.

DAUGHTER. That's not a fight with yourself, that's what they call "a party."

FATHER. Ah.

DAUGHTER. They're unfortunate, aren't they?

FATHER. Parties? Depends if your friends are there…

DAUGHTER. Yes, but we don't have any friends.

FATHER. You're right parties are awful.

DAUGHTER. There's something very abrupt about parties where you don't know anyone.

FATHER. Yes.

DAUGHTER. You're suddenly thrust into an artificial environment where you have to convince people that you're worthwhile–

FATHER. Yes.

DAUGHTER. I find it difficult because I lack "a charming switch."

FATHER. As do I.

DAUGHTER. I am fully aware that I'm wonderful, but I want to show it to people when I jolly well please. And not before.

FATHER. So don't go to parties.

DAUGHTER. I won't, they're stupid.

FATHER. Yes, they are.

DAUGHTER. I'd rather sit at home and appreciate myself, or something.

FATHER. Yeah, or watch bad T.V.

DAUGHTER. Yeah.

(beat)

FATHER. You know when you go on a vacation to a new place and people make you do things?

DAUGHTER. Yeah. I hate that.

FATHER. I do too, they say, "Go explore, see the city," when the reality is that you don't speak the language, you are completely alone, you don't have very much money and you hate yourself for going there in the first place. It's like Paris, Paris is the worst place in the world.

DAUGHTER. I agree, it's the worst place in the world.

FATHER. It's like, yeah, so it's pretty, can I go home now? And the people…

DAUGHTER. But people are nice, sometimes.

FATHER. Yeah, people are nice sometimes, your grandmother was nice.

DAUGHTER. I'm sure she was. But most people are a pointless nightmare.

FATHER. YES, most people are a pointless nightmare–

DAUGHTER. It's like school.

FATHER. Yes, it is like school.

DAUGHTER. School is like a party that never ends, so people start to eat each other.

FATHER. Don't forget the homework.

DAUGHTER. Yes, yes, with homework, so you can't forget about the constant filth you are being subjected to.

FATHER. I believe the whole idea of school is to ensure that that filth stays with you.

DAUGHTER. You're right there is a terrifying permanence about the education system. The whole idea being that you get there in the morning, and you can never leave.

FATHER. Yes, it's constant isn't it? A constant reminder. Like a kippah,

DAUGHTER. Yeah, like a kippah.

(beat)

FATHER. Is that why you're here?

DAUGHTER. Yes, that's why I'm here.

FATHER. You're bored.

DAUGHTER. Yes, I'm bored.

FATHER. That's why you want love.

DAUGHTER. I suppose it is.

FATHER. Love is to you, what a kippah is to our people.

DAUGHTER. A reminder of, what?

FATHER. A reminder that life isn't such a complete waste of time. I had it, and now that it's gone I am completely lacking that reminder.

DAUGHTER. Sure, but at least you know it exists.

FATHER. Maybe.

DAUGHTER. Definitely! You have proof!

FATHER. It left.

DAUGHTER. Yeah…

FATHER. I'm sorry you're bored.

DAUGHTER. Thank you.

FATHER. Better to be bored than to be bore-ing.

DAUGHTER. You're right.

FATHER. They say the only people that can be bored are boring people, but boring people are always doing things.

DAUGHTER. That's true, they're always, like, talking to each other.

FATHER. Yeah, or at the mall.

DAUGHTER. Yeah.

FATHER. It's the geniuses that never have anything to do.

DAUGHTER. Really?

FATHER. Sure, they don't have an overwhelming amount of people of their caliber to be in contact with.

DAUGHTER. Hm.

(beat)

FATHER. You'll get over it you know.

DAUGHTER. What?

FATHER. Being bored.

DAUGHTER. I will?

FATHER. Oh, sure, one day you'll get out of that hell-hole that they call the education system and do something important with your time.

DAUGHTER. Yes, but what if I never fall in love?

FATHER. Well, then you'll die alone. But I can guarantee you'll have some laughs.

DAUGHTER. Thanks for that.

FATHER. You're gonna be just fine. In my life, alone I have seen more than a few interesting things.

DAUGHTER. What where they?

FATHER. I can't remember, but I'm sure they happened.

DAUGHTER. Well as long as you're sure.

   (beat)

FATHER. Will you remember me when I die?

DAUGHTER. I think if my memory is up to par it would be impossible for me to forget you.

FATHER. Nice to know.

DAUGHTER. Have you ever met a ghost?

FATHER. Certainly.

DAUGHTER. I wonder if you'll be a ghost.

FATHER. You can't be a ghost unless your life is unfinished.

DAUGHTER. How do you mean?

FATHER. If you've left something behind. Ghosts are the dead returning to take care of the unfinished.

DAUGHTER. Then, I wouldn't like you to be a ghost.

FATHER. No.

DAUGHTER. Even if I missed you, I'd like you to rest when you're dead.

FATHER. Thank you.

DAUGHTER. That's all being dead is good for really.

FATHER. Mm.

DAUGHTER. I used to think there was something so final about dying.

FATHER. It's final if you're lucky.

(beat)

DAUGHTER. What did it say?

FATHER. What?

DAUGHTER. You said you met a ghost, what did it say?

FATHER. Oh, nothing. I suppose it didn't want anything with me.

DAUGHTER. You think they only talk to you if they want something?

FATHER. Why should they talk to you otherwise? The living are not their concern unless they need something from them.

DAUGHTER. Hm.

(beat)

FATHER. Why don't you go back to sleep?

DAUGHTER. I can't or I'll never sleep tonight.

FATHER. How do you know?

DAUGHTER. Because you cant "go" to sleep you have to "fall" asleep, which takes an enormous amount of sub-conscious effort.

FATHER. Why subconscious?

DAUGHTER. Because if it were conscious you would give yourself an aneurysm as opposed to the need to shut your eyes. That's what happens when you think about it too much.

FATHER. Yeah I suppose forced relaxation isn't relaxation at all.

DAUGHTER. No, of course not, it's having a panic attack on the massage table.

FATHER. Yes. It's like me. I can't enjoy anything, I should just end it all.

(beat)

DAUGHTER. You don't mean that do you?

FATHER. No, I was just being dramatic.

DAUGHTER. Oh, good.

FATHER. I'm sorry, I didn't mean to upset you.

DAUGHTER. It's alright, but I hope you know that I like having you around.

FATHER. Thank you.

DAUGHTER. And I'd prefer you to enjoy yourself.

FATHER. Thank you.

DAUGHTER. And funerals.

FATHER. Oh, yeah I wouldn't want to put you through my funeral.

DAUGHTER. Oh no it's not that, they're just so expensive, it's the paying for it that would upset me.

FATHER. I expected no less. Anyway I take it back, what I said, I take it all back.

DAUGHTER. Thank you.

FATHER. Well, I'd like to be around someday when, you, god-willing, have children.

DAUGHTER. You forget that I'm never going to fall in love.

FATHER. Doesn't necessarily mean you can't be a slut!

DAUGHTER. That's true.

FATHER. I'm sure your children would be very lovely.

DAUGHTER. Sure they would, slutty people always make the cutest babies.

FATHER. It's interesting that you have spent an average amount of time on this earth, and that's the piece of information that you come away with.

DAUGHTER. Well, I might learn other things.

FATHER. That's true.

DAUGHTER. I might teach my children other things.

FATHER. Such as?

DAUGHTER. I don't know. How to not be an insufferable person.

FATHER. Well, that's a good start. In fact I think that's all that parenting really is.

DAUGHTER. Did you like it?

FATHER. Did I like what, parenting?

DAUGHTER. Yes.

FATHER. Well I shouldn't like to think it's over yet.

DAUGHTER. No, of course not, I meant, *do* you like it.

FATHER. Well it might get a little awkward if I said I didn't don't you think?

DAUGHTER. I suppose so.

FATHER. Do you know what it's like?

DAUGHTER. No.

FATHER. I'll tell you what it's like.

DAUGHTER. What's it like?

FATHER. It's nice.

DAUGHTER. Well that sounds nice. Maybe I'll have them.

    (beat)

DAUGHTER. I shouldn't like to be pregnant, though.

FATHER. What? You mean right now? I shouldn't like that either.

DAUGHTER. No, I mean, in general…

FATHER. Oh.

DAUGHTER. Have you ever seen *A Place in the Sun?*

FATHER. Of course.

DAUGHTER. Well, I'm afraid I'm going to turn into that.

FATHER. Into what, Monty Clift?

DAUGHTER. No, into Shelly Winters.

FATHER. What?

DAUGHTER. I'm afraid I'll grow up to be the annoying pregnant girl everybody wants to murder.

FATHER. Ah, I see. But you'd much rather be Elizabeth Taylor.

DAUGHTER. Yes.

FATHER. Because she is, as you put it, "a wounded heart?"

DAUGHTER. Yes. And she's pretty.

FATHER. And also there's that.

DAUGHTER. Yes.

FATHER. Well I can understand why you don't wish to be known as that homely girl that men feel like drowning.

DAUGHTER. Do you?

FATHER. Yes, but I don't really think it's anything to worry about.

DAUGHTER. No?

FATHER. No. I think, as I shall put it in light words, you have an "artistic temperament," which you most certainly got from me.

DAUGHTER. What does that mean?

FATHER. It means you're an insane, hysterical human being and you should probably just calm down.

DAUGHTER. I suppose what you mean to tell me is that I have an active mind?

FATHER. Yes, that is exactly what I mean. An active mind is both a blessing and a curse.

DAUGHTER. In that–what?

FATHER. In that you can probably write a decent poem and you will spend the majority of your time hating yourself and wanting to rip all your hair out.

DAUGHTER. Thank you, I'll keep that in mind.

FATHER. But you must not do that, you understand.

DAUGHTER. Why?

FATHER. Because what you do not realize, is that in spite of all that paranoia and self-loathing you are actually quite a wonderful, remarkable person. You just don't feel that way because you're Jewish.

(beat)

DAUGHTER. Well, better to be that than the other thing.

FATHER. It took me half a lifetime to figure that out, I'm glad you've come to that conclusion early on. You might even be able to enjoy yourself.

DAUGHTER. I certainly hope so.

FATHER. As you should.

DAUGHTER. I'd like to grow up to be proud of myself.

FATHER. Undoubtedly you will.

DAUGHTER. I hope you're right.

FATHER. I know I'm right.

(beat)

DAUGHTER. People tell me that it's wrong to want to be successful.

FATHER. Those people are fools.

DAUGHTER. I suppose so. But what is the mark of a fool?

FATHER. An idiot.

DAUGHTER. Ah. But it's more than that. It's a step past stupidity, being a fool is the polar opposite of wisdom.

FATHER. And they're douchebags.

DAUGHTER. That too.

FATHER. Like you're boy, he is undoubtedly a fool because, he's in…I don't know, art school? Wasting his parent's money without even a thought to his profession. And he let you go, which makes him a douchebag.

DAUGHTER. But he's so cute.

FATHER. Cuteness is a genetic abnormality that allows the animal in question to feed off the host.

DAUGHTER. Are you sure you don't want any coffee?

FATHER. I can't drink caffeine anymore. Feeling happy and shaky at the same time makes me feel like a drug addict.

DAUGHTER. Or a small town girl in the big city?

FATHER. Yes, both are undesirable.

DAUGHTER. Yes, in fact I think both are on my list.

FATHER. What list?

DAUGHTER. I've started making lists of things I hate. It's my hobby.

FATHER. You have a hobby?

DAUGHTER. I got tired of telling people I didn't have a hobby. So now my hobby is making lists of things I hate.

FATHER. And how is that going?

DAUGHTER. It makes me feel jaded, old, snide and opinionated, it's going excellently.

FATHER. Glad to hear it, what's first on your list?

DAUGHTER. People that don't laugh at my jokes.

FATHER. Agreed. Those people disgust me.

DAUGHTER. Yes. Clearly no sense of humor.

FATHER. Yes…and they're stupid.

DAUGHTER. Yes.

FATHER. What's second on your list?

DAUGHTER. People that laugh at *all* my jokes.

FATHER. Those people disgust me to!

DAUGHTER. I don't understand why they would feel the need to laugh at every single one of them, it's like, must you?

FATHER. Yeah, and they're stupid.

DAUGHTER. Yeah.

FATHER. Stupid people would be on my list.

DAUGHTER. Yes.

FATHER. You know why?

DAUGHTER. Because they're stupid?

FATHER. Exactly.

(beat)

DAUGHTER. I forget, sometimes all the things that I know.

FATHER. You're old enough to know better and young enough not to care.

DAUGHTER. But I wish I didn't do that.

FATHER. Oh sure you do.

DAUGHTER. You're right, it's enormously fun to feel sorry for myself.

FATHER. Exactly. You have the luxury of being dismayed at the state of the world and horrified at what you have turned into, and then you can chat with your friends in the back of geometry.

DAUGHTER. And I don't have to pay taxes.

FATHER. Also very true.

DAUGHTER. And you!

FATHER. And I, what?

DAUGHTER. You have the luxury of saying whatever you want to anyone because your wife left you! And you get to hang around in bars wearing flannel and looking sad!

DAUGHTER. Yes.

FATHER. Yes.

DAUGHTER. Yes.

(beat)

FATHER. Now I have something to say.

DAUGHTER. Alright.

FATHER. One day you're going to leave me and fall in love. You're smart. You know that. And until that day comes, do me a favor and try not to worry so much.

DAUGHTER. Okay.

FATHER. And don't go back to school.

DAUGHTER. You're right. I won't.

FATHER. Good.

DAUGHTER. Now will you do me a favor?

FATHER. Sure.

DAUGHTER. Don't talk about dying so much. It upsets me.

FATHER. Does it?

DAUGHTER. Yes, as I said you're important to have around.

FATHER. Mm.

DAUGHTER. And I would like you to be happy, for my sake, it would make me happy.

FATHER. You're absolutely right, I owe you an apology.

DAUGHTER. Accepted.

FATHER. Well then, I promise.

DAUGHTER. Thank you.

(beat)

FATHER. You're young, you'll get over it.

DAUGHTER. You'll get over it too. It's always the worst until it's not anymore.

FATHER. My dear you're an eternal optimist.

DAUGHTER. I love you very much, you know.

FATHER. I love you too.

DAUGHTER. Please, have some coffee.

FATHER. Well perhaps just this once.

THE END

www.ingramcontent.com/pod-product-compliance
Lightning Source LLC
Chambersburg PA
CBHW051413290426
44108CB00015B/2272